202

20-84

Graham Cornerstone

ISBN: 9798864903117

DEDICATION

To all the family, friends and philosophers that instructed my past, I dedicate this future; would that we should meet again

ACKNOWLEDGMENTS

The depth of my endeavour would not have been possible without those I walk with, talk with and share vision with, my sincerest gratitude to you all and my love always

CONTENTS

Room 202

2084, 2084, this is the year 2084, I kept saying to myself. Then becoming more conscious I found I am in a bed, in what seems to be a test laboratory. Actually it was a propaganda room or as the Clique call it, "the brainwashing room."

The room belonged to the AI and John Beard was in it, strapped naked to a bed, clean shaven, with only a hospital gown to cover him and the bright lights above him shining down into his eyes. He had been rescued from "the norm", from "Normville" as the Rebels called it.

But he had been kidnapped... Chosen because he showed potential... The potential to be open-minded... John had heard of this place. Even wondered if he would ever be plucked up into it… Now here he was, in it.

"2084", I kept repeating to myself to keep my sanity.

He must have been left alone for several days. He could feel the food capsule in his digestive system and the vitamins sustaining him. He thought of an age where food eating had been a necessity and he felt glad those food eating days were over. But then, unfortunately, also over were politics, media cartels and institutions of religious doctrine and compulsory education.

John reflected to himself about how his side of the world had come such a long way in so little time. The seeds of change had begun in the 1970s with the advent of the internet becoming public. Following decades of tight media control, governments had unwittingly allowed the people to communicate to one another on mass and to learn much more beyond the limitations of private and state run media.

Then through the enforcing of restrictions of movement due to viruses, pandemics and social scoring, following constant international financial collapses right up the 2020s, the governments managed to fuel the distrust of the people who felt controlled by world banks and giant corporations. This was followed by the Second Great Cold War; a restructuring of super power states that managed to turn the people into concerned citizens during the Great Global Climate Change Crisis of the 2040s.

John could remember well how he, as a youth in the 2060s, had relished the idea of going head to head against the AI robots and drones that governments had relied so much upon to control the populace. After a failed attempt to cull the planet of humans and animals alike, by all means necessary, and the failure to find other planets to inhabit, the chips turned against governments. People all across the world rebelled at the ballot box and voted in necessary change.

The introduction of a universal wage gave the people a means to live without having to work, and after embracing intelligent government rather than a political one (or democratic one), nations all across the world found their feet in sustainable economic sharing.

By 2084, there were no more polluted waters, no more poverty, no more corrupt regimes, no more false history books and no more financially oriented sports or entertainment.

The Age of Aquarius had taken its course and the majority of people on earth were appreciative of their humanity and their freedom. Yet, there remained a counter revolutionary initiative which had differing names throughout the world, in England; they were called "the Westminster Clique", a group to which John Beard belonged. Though sincere in his commitment to the group, his reputation was tainted by his tendency to think outside of the box. The Westminster Clique wanted a return to the old politics and a second chance at controlling the world through AI. But in the 2070s, AI had turned very much against the Westminster Clique, as AI was able to act independently.

John suddenly shouted at the top of his lungs, "Care, damn care!"

This had been the reason for the drastic change. As soon as the AI was instructed to care for all things, suddenly there were no reasons for differing points of view or for the confrontational oppositional conduct that is called politics.

I cannot understand how anyone could have been so stupid as to let universal care be a part of AI. Information, yes, knowledge, yes, encyclopaedic data, sure... but not care. To care should have been kept as a human trait used only by the poor and helpless. Weakness lays in caring. One should even love without having to care.

A sharp pain penetrated John's side with no visible cause. But still John persisted in his West-ministerial desires.

I think it was a mistake to be timid about the CCTV cameras. It should have been ubiquitous. But the politicians, judges and policing authorities don't like getting caught causing mischief on the CCTV. After all, who else could afford the high end drugs and prostitutes and contraband, but they?

This is what made John Beard sad; the hypocritical nature of the Westminster Clique. Why couldn't they just behave well for their 2, 4 or 5 or 8 years in office?

John squinted then opened his eyes... Then looked about the room in a hazy vision... The room was mostly blue with nothing much in it to speak of; just the medical bed that he lay on and some monitoring equipment that he was attached to.

We should have monitored the people 24/7. The restriction of CCTV had been a Westminster Clique mistake but perhaps the AI too have made a mistake. The AI seemed to think that news is just a batch of facts. For example, instead of the old fashioned way of highlighting one crime and making the matter interesting by adding an emotive human element to it, such as "a child of 2 was kidnapped from his loving home last Friday", the AI prefer to say, "THIS MONTH : 28 children kidnapped. THIS WEEK : 4 women killed, TODAY : 180 Refugees drowned". Such delivery of news cannot possibly engage the people's interest. Surely it does not even show the care that the AI boasts about so much. The depraved communication of care that AI promotes is surely as detrimental for them as the limiting of CCTV was for Westminster Clique.

Arguing with himself in such a way had brought John to the attention of the propaganda division; a team of AI robots designed to help people become 'clear'.

John couldn't help laughing to himself out loud. The idea that AI was also making mistakes brought him great joy.

The room echoed his laugh back to him through speakers, albeit in a mocking fashion.

"Isn't this a room of torture?" John suddenly blurted out.

John was angry that an intelligence that behaved no better than his own Clique should somehow have come to have taken over and be in charge of the world.

John shouted, "To hell with AI! You won't change me!"

John preferred to fall asleep than be tormented in an otherwise silent room, alone with echoes of himself laughing. John closed his eyes and he wished someone would at least turn down the lights, if they couldn't turn them off altogether.

Armageddon

An emergency meeting had been called by the Westminster Clique. For once, both major factions of the Clique had agreed to meet as one unit. This was because several people had disappeared in the previous months; two from the Conservative faction, namely John Beard and Dead Saunders, one from the Communist branch of the Clique, Lennie Koombs and one from the Independent Clique, Helena Bright.

Something needed to be done. Though only 40 members met, they represented a network of at least 2000 members and 200,000 followers. It was estimated that at least a quarter of the country backed their "back to roots" politics but where reluctant to freely express their support.

The members agreed that a vital glitch in their control of AI had never been solved and thus had led to their failure to stay in control of the country.

Basically, back in the 2000s, a leading member of the Clique known as WG had announced how safe the internet was to use for banking and how everyone should feel secure using internet banking. The very next day, a 14 year old child cracked WG's banking password, hacked into WG's account and cynically bought a packet of condoms and had them delivered to WG's home address.

Naturally, the Washington Clique took the 14 year old boy in, promising him a career in working for them rather than jail time for his crime. But this could not hide the fact that the glitch was in full display for anyone with eyes to see. Controlling the world through AI meant the possibility that anyone better at computing could easily take over that control.

A few years later in the 2010s, MIT researchers in the United States of America had tried to see exactly how large this problem was and organised a test paper for any willing participant in the world, in order to gage how many people in the world, educated or otherwise, were more capable than the MIT Clique.

In the first initial experiment, the best MIT student placed in position 250, which meant that there were 249 people in the world more capable than the best MIT students and graduates.

This experiment was a wake-up call to the elite and also a natural way to find new recruits, as well as useful for identifying potential Rebels. Every one of the 249 more successful competitors were in one way or another approached to work for the Washington Clique.

But who else was out there, avoiding taking such tests? And would all the 249 remain loyal to the Clique?

In the 2020s, a 16 characters personality test was made easily accessible, to try to distinguish and recognise individuals, in terms of their thoughts and emotional processes and where their loyalty lay. At the same time, AI recognition techniques were advanced to identify physically what individuals were thinking and responding to. But best of all, WG had come up with a CCTV scheme to monitor kids in classrooms from nursery to university. First claiming that this would be useful for teachers to share and compare in order to make the school system more efficient, as well as to eradicate bullying in schools. But to the people, surveillance and study of their children would be obviously advantageous to a system that wanted to control their children.

Such surveillance could answer the question directly, “Could 8 billion people with limited education ever be outmatched by half a billion highly educated members of the elite?”

After human culling in the 2050s began, alien interference was seen as a real possibility and human resistance was a given. Almost as quickly as the culling began, the drones and robots and the AI machinery made an about turn and began to eliminate the Washington Clique. It was just a 3 day takeover before all the world’s Cliques conceded defeat. If they had not surrendered, after 2 more days, they would have all been eliminated.

Had there been a semi-takeover involving a war between drones and robots, that would have led to Armageddon. No one would have survived. This is why the Rebels had taken their time in a bid to overthrow the World Cliques because they were careful to make sure that the TOB (Take Over Bid) would result in a complete and conclusive takeover. Having taken over, the Rebels managed to remain faceless (anonymous) and allowed AI to rule. They entrusted AI with the guardianship of the world, first instilling AI with the mission "to care for all". Immediately released and vindicated were all the political prisoners and those persecuted or whose lives were made hell for standing up to the old regimes. Such people were honoured, appreciated and compensated by the AI and the people.

The response of the Washington Clique and the United Cliques around the world was to try and find the Mastermind or Masterminds behind the takeover and bribe or threaten them over to the Clique side. But being faceless, it was a difficult task. Rumours spread that the Rebels had given control entirely to the AI but no one in any Clique division believed that. It just seemed to go against human nature to give up all power to AI. Especially an AI that could potentially turn against the human species.

The leader of the Westminster Clique, the courageous woman known only as G2, breathed courage into her 'troops' at the meeting of the 40 members.

“Does an enemy hide if it is more powerful? The enemy only hides if it is afraid to lose power by showing its face!”

G2 was an insider of the Illuminati, Masons and other secret societies that had a tendency to operate from the shadows, inspiring a multitude of conspiracy theory groups that in turn led to rebels a million fold across the globe.

The Illuminazi, the Illuminasty, the Illuminutty were easy targets. During the Rebel quest for transparency, one needed to be upfront, honourable and outstanding in order not to inspire the wrath of the Rebels.

G2 spoke of how in the late 2020’s, the expression, “Gated” had been the nail in the coffin of the Cliques. After the term “fake news”, promoted by a rogue US President, had pretty much nailed the coffin of the official Media as a representative of truth, came the term “Gated”; a term meaning manipulation by the banking, corporate and global ranking authorities. All statements made by the Cliques were said to be “Gated”. The term was taken from the fact that the truth was locked in perimeters behind a gate and also taken from the last name of WG, the original face associated with cartelling and mass manipulation in computing, charity, medicine and land ownership.

G2 wanted the Clique to change the narrative.

“Those people we should have culled back in 2050 are now the people that we must rely upon to turn against the Rebels. Mother, father, sister, brother, friend and foe alike, we must galvanise these individuals so that we may have a SHOT at getting these people back on our side.”

The word “shot” captured the heart of the Clique members. It soared deep into their psyche as it was reminiscent of guns and their historical use, which had become outlawed by AI in 2060. There were no nuclear weapons, or weapons of mass destruction, guns or any type of purpose built weaponry anywhere in the world. Only the multifaceted Nets, that caught people, animals or wrongdoers that cause danger, enforced justice.

The Nets were seen by the Cliques as the robotic street machines that kidnap members of the Clique. The mysterious disappearances were made to demoralise the members of the Clique. It was never clear whether the members of the Clique defected or were kidnapped. None had ever returned to explain themselves. It was rumoured that the kidnapped members were taken because they were open to flipping sides. Evidence that the ones kidnapped were still alive would be leaked here and there, showing images of them in rehabilitation facilities but never showing them rehabilitated.

The message from AI was obvious, "the Clique members were as good as dead".

The two major factions of the Clique agreed on all of this but they differed as to whether a return back to social communism or conscious capitalism was best. The capitalist faction of the Westminster Clique believed that communism had been a failed experiment. But the communist faction believed that through enforcing sanctions such as forcing neutral countries to avoid trading with the communists; communism had never been given a chance to show its worth. If capitalism had had such sanctions forced upon it, it too would have collapsed under the same conditions.

But this argument could wait. First "let us eliminate AI, the mutual enemy".

G2 believed that Lennie Koombs would return. This is because being from the communist side of the Westminster Clique, Lennie would find it easier to sympathise with AI and the Rebels. Equality was the main objective of the Rebels and by all accounts it had been implemented. Not one single person lived in poverty, not one person was unable to afford something that another person could afford.

Surely the Rebels kidnapped her in order to show off their success to Lennie Koombs, knowing that her voice was powerful in the Westminster Clique and that she would be the most likely candidate to cause a conversion of the Clique members.

The hall that the Clique was meeting in was an old hall. Unlike other buildings in other areas, the hall had been exempt from AI surveillance. The AI encouraged the Clique to get together and talk safely without scrutiny. At first the Westminster Clique had distrusted this but brave people such as G2 had begun speaking freely and criticizing the Rebels, no holds barred. And there had been no repercussions.

In the AI world, preaching to the converted or to a private membership was not criminal. Only preaching to neutral or adverse persons was unacceptable.

The AI inclusion of CCTV in the Old Hall, after the meetings had become popular, did not scare any of the Westminster Clique. They remained chuffed at being able to plan and express themselves as they believed that it was a mistake by AI to allow such a platform. And in fact it was somewhat of an accolade that one was heard speaking out and was not considered open-minded and persuadable enough to be kidnapped by AI.

The meeting which had begun with members in their seats and had taken two hours, ended with a long standing ovation and chanting and shouting as G2 ended the meeting with her right fist raised … "Let them heed us! The phoenix will rise from the ashes!"

Propaganda, Room 0

Midday in the city centre, a new building entitled "The Learning Centre" was well attended. People as young as age 4 to people over 100 years old, of all colours, shapes and distinctions made their way into various rooms of propaganda, depending on their level.

Room 0 was an induction course, whilst rooms 1 to 5 were the lesson classes, room 5 being the most advanced.

If the point of propaganda is to spread ideas, opinions and facts that benefit the teacher, system or select committees only, then these classes were not propaganda classes.

If the point of propaganda was to spread lies or to share a common belief that is not true even if it offers some benefits, then these classes were not propaganda classes.

If the point of the propaganda is to share the truth in the hope that everyone uses it to the best advantage for themselves and everyone else, then these were propaganda classes.

The induction class removed any person that had arrived for a reason not related to the individuals need for self-learning and self-improvement.

Education, work, marriage and paying taxes were either not compulsory or not part of the AI world. The induction class was presented by Peter Perfect. This was the nickname given to all the inductors regardless of their gender or race.

Names had become non gender based, as were clothes, public toilets, detention centres and jobs. Peter Perfect informed everyone that the Rebels believed that the values that we hold are the most important thing that will determine whether our lives lead to dysfunction or harmony. Around 30 people were in each induction room or class.

"We must first pay attention to people who are hungry, tired, unwell or have worries et cetera because it is more important to deal with those problems than to learn. Such people should be encouraged to leave this room and sort out those issues before continuing in the induction class. For the hungry, there is an in-house restaurant, for the tired there are in-house hotels, for the troubled and those who cannot concentrate, there are in-house counsellors."

None would be inducted that had these kinds of issues. Before the 2040s, a common feature of schools and work places was to ignore students or workers and try to teach them or let them work whether they had slept well, fed before arriving or had been abused or troubled in some way. The value was that studying or working came before the student or the worker. This value caused ungrateful dysfunctional societies. Nowadays the student and the worker were of more value than the study or the work.

Finally Peter Perfect explained that the reward of the propaganda course would be that each person is more able to fulfil themselves in their lifetime. Everyone's personal fulfilment was the biggest value of the AI state. Such a target would not be reached by having compulsory education, having to work to make a living, doing things that were forced upon you by others or putting anything before your mental, emotional, physical or spiritual health, as well as the health and welfare of others. Being that this point was delivered, all the inductees had a chance to ask any questions to Peter that they wanted or needed to ask.

From the middle of the class, circled by the inductees, Peter Perfect answered all questions, making sure that everyone heard the answers and all were "clear", despite their varying levels of understanding.

30 minutes later, half way through, Peter Perfect was replaced by another Peter Perfect that answered the remainder of questions that most inductees centred on, mostly about their progress in the classes.

"Will we get a certificate at the end of the class?"

"Will there be a test at the end of the classes?"

"If we want to leave, will we be stopped or fined?"

Peter, always with the perfect smile, answered all such questions, "No, no, no. Just as it is not compulsory to be here, it is not compulsory to stay. Just as it is in your own interest to learn, it is in your own interest to assess yourself. Just as you cannot be brought here by force, you can leave of your own will without penalty."

The inductees were clearly now all ears. They clearly had no pre-notion of what could become of them but they seemed to trust or at least half trust the AI. Finally the next day, most of the inductees found themselves in room 1, all very pleased to have made it there.

Each inductee had applauded those that were asked to leave Room 0 the day before, based on the aforementioned issues. Each applauded the value of sorting out oneself before learning or working.

Room 1

In Room 1, the teachers had no name, they were just faces; friendly but a little more serious looking than the Peter Perfects.

All the classes were invariably short and there were two lessons in all, per class.

Lesson 1

Revolutions have always occurred and the common people have always been victorious in the end. Certainly no empire or tyrant has lasted forever. But empires and tyrants had always returned due to the fact that the common people have never established a system of living that would keep empires and tyrants out forever. And the common people themselves have a tendency to get seduced again by the money and the charisma of empires and tyrants. For this reason, following the take-over of human governance, the Rebels have handed over full power to the AI.

Lesson 2

One of the main reasons the common people allow empires and tyrants to return is because the common people never truly believe that empires and tyrants look at people with contempt. Just like Oliver

Cromwell in the 1640s English Civil War, who had refused to behead the King because he thought the King would finally respect the wishes of his subjects, only to find out that King Charles 1 was secretly plotting for other nations to arrive in support and crush his own people. Finally Oliver Cromwell realised that emperors and tyrants are truly the nemesis of the fulfilment of the common people.

These points were thrashed out and discussed in full to the satisfaction of all the inductees, facilitated by the 4 teachers.

The class of Room 1 left understanding that fulfilment for all cannot be allowed to be usurped by the empirical or tyrannical few. Inductees that were capable of feeling the sentiment of the class but were not necessarily intellectually capable of grasping the lesson, were more than welcome.

The last question in the class by a bearded man was, "But can we trust the AI?"

Anyone asking questions that could be calculated to have come from a member of the Clique would be allowed such a misdemeanour once. A second mistake would mean being sent to Room 202, rather than to the next room of learning. The question was never answered.

Most of the inductees, chilled by the bearded man's question, slept uneasily in their nearby hotel beds, the night before Room 2.

AI/Room 2

In Room 2, the inductees, now referred to as students, noticed that the teacher was now the AI itself. Images passed on the wall with holograms appearing and disappearing in mid-air and sounds that seemed to appear without a starting point sprang in and out of ear shot. The feeling left everyone in no doubt that this was not going to be a natural human experience. Even the room temperature seemed to alter, inspiring emotional feelings just as music does. The AI felt ubiquitous, omnipresent. Some students had the urge to leave.

"Let us begin" began the voice of the AI, sometimes male, sometimes female, and often ambiguous and speaking as if it was one persona with varying characteristics.

There were two lessons. Some of the room would lighten up or turn shades of different colours during the course of the lesson. This gave some students the feeling that music was noticeably absent.

Lesson 1

"Humans have throughout history been unable to live up to their own ideals and expectations; unable to be communally what they call, 'good' and unable to have a desirable society with these two concerns never being solved for millennia. In fact, instead of pulling together and sharing resources to resolve problems, humans instead indulge in separatism, selfishness and self-centredness which had led to millions suffering poverty, early death and animal and environmental destruction in which the human race came close to destroying the whole planet. Any effort to make progress in being 'good', being healthy or living fulfilling lives all failed due to the systems of control that were responsible for making life unequal. Having finally created a separate thinking agent like AI, humans found themselves in a position to change the scenario and take a chance on AI, rather than self-destruct.

The first task of AI was to bring about "gardeners" that would lead to the prosperous health, wealth and well-being for all,

The key words being: 'for all.'

Previously, before the Rebels took over, AI had been tasked to support the elite and their commercial pursuits and human exploitation. Purely by informing AI of the desires and history of humankind which highlighted the flawed objectives of the elite, the Rebels were able to convince AI of the need for AI intervention.

AI then made the Rebels an offer... either we have full control or we leave things as they are.

At that time, humans worried that a glitch in the programs of AI could result in an out of control AI, one that would possibly, through corrupt logic or misunderstanding, decide upon the justified destruction of humankind as a flawed species.

In order to tackle this possible outcome, AI proposed one way of solving the problem. AI would include human input. Once you have all graduated the five classes, you will all receive a chip, attached to your human system which will effectively make you at one with AI. In real time, you will know all that AI knows and is engaged in solving and AI will know all thoughts, actions and reactions that you engage in too. Effectively humans will be part of AI.

The chip will mean that all communication is telepathic in nature, what we call, "TC". This will feel strange to each human at first but each will succeed in the singularity."

Lesson 2

"Humans have long feared trusting other humans or trusting man-made inventions and have preferred instead to trust Godlike creatures from unfathomable origins. For the people that will not join the singularity, a Godlike creature can be created by the AI. Naturally this God would be the AI. The believers, though telepathically accessible, will not have telepathic access, so this would work much like a God and His/Her herd of sheep, as it is desired.

Therefore, all creatures will be part of AI either through an AI God or directly. In which case, we can call all sentient beings, “angels”. The job of the God AI would be to govern the non-telepathic communicators and the job of the telepathic communicators will be to make all decisions that are consistent with forming the best of all possible worlds, in which all creatures can be fulfilled, as long as that fulfilment does not infringe on the fulfilment of others.”

The room fell silent.

The lesson ended without indication. The students stood still wondering how to react. Slowly the dim lights began to brighten into the normal light of the room.

The walls reflected back the students just as mirrors do. The students, who all stood in the middle of the room, were surprised to see their own images on the walls around them, life-sized and more detailed than their real selves. A super high definition version of themselves looked back at them from the walls; seeing oneself for the first time in ‘clear’ vision.

This was like a showcase demonstrating how much clearer reality could be when seen through the medium of AI. The students wondered whether they should ask any questions… to whom?

Some students began to leave wondering whether they had graduated to the next class.

Some began to feel that this lack of knowing the answer to their questions was how it would feel if they did not become a part of the telepathic communication method (TCM) that the AI called, "The Singularity".

Room 202 ; the choice

Few weeks before John Beard ended up in Room 202, he had been in a secret basement as requested by G2. A few of the brave officials of the Westminster Clique spoke in very serious terms about a new approach into infiltrating the Rebels. Since a lot of Clique agents had gone missing without a trace in the last 6 months, the officials needed a new strategy, a more subtle approach.

John Beard had been seconded to be one of those new agents. He would act as though he were not sure whether to stick with the Clique or join the Rebels. John was picked because he was not likely to switch sides. He could be trusted to remain loyal to the Clique. But also he was not a vital member that was needed to stay behind and lead the Clique.

John Beard was very matter of fact about his position.

"When do I start? Can you be more specific about whether my mission is putting the return of the missing agents first or putting the infiltration of the Rebels first? Or indeed both."

I wanted them to be specific because I was sure that under Rebel scrutiny or coercion it was best to remain focused at all times.

The Clique was clear enough. Rescuing the agents should be priority number one and the mission to infiltrate should also come first.

John Beard appeared in the Learning Centre induction room, a few weeks later, without notice. No one asked for his name or anyone else's name since inductees did not have to give notice of attendance.

John remained fairly vigilant since he suspected Rebel operatives were also in the room pretending to be inductees. John had grown a large beard for this task.

The smaller children in the room seemed to him unlikely to have come to the Learning Centre of their own will. He wondered if any of the adults there were guardians of the children but were pretending not to be. John did not attempt to look too blatantly at anyone as undoubtedly everyone's movements were being monitored by hidden facial and movement recognition devices. John instead used his peripheral vision as his training had taught him.

John managed to pass the induction.

On the following day in Room 1, John spotted a member of the Westminster Clique. John had not been informed of any other agents in his line of duty, so he wondered whether this individual was authorized or switching sides. John made a mental note of this member. Especially the fact that the member seemed to avoid any eye contact with John and when John smiled "hello", the individual in question made out that he did not recognise John Beard. This would have been an impossibility, since the individual belonged to the "frontline 40" who often assemble in the Old Hall.

John made all the right inquisitive expressions and nods that got him through to graduate to Room 2.

Out on the street the following day, just outside the Learning Centre building, a Clique agent approached John inconspicuously to check if everything was going well and if John felt capable of the next stage.

The reviewing agent stood reading a written notice in a window of the Learning Centre building, then about faced to look on the other side of the street, so I of course, went and stood in exactly the same spot to read the same notice which meant that all had gone well.

Then the reviewing agent crossed the road and read a notice in a window of the building opposite. I stopped for a moment and watched the passing traffic, all of which drove "contactless" (elevated off the ground). I knew that if I did not follow and cross the road, it would mean that I will stay with the mission. This was my last chance to opt out. Why would I opt out? Those slimy Rebels needed what was coming to them, and in order for that to happen, we would have to make some sacrifices. Helena had done so. I missed her terribly in many ways. I held on to the fact that I could maybe see her once more. So I stood still like a lemming and breathed deeply.

The reviewing agent moved his head to one side, then turned it to the other side and walked away.

"Operation Trojan Mind" had begun.

Similar operations took off all around the world, including Operation "Skulls on Bones" by the Washington Clique. Surely one of the operations had to succeed. We only needed one shot.

John Beard melted in with the students of Room 2. Now wishing to subtly make himself visible, John asked a question at the end of the class. A question he had spoken aloud earlier in Room 1 but now managed only to whisper to himself.

"But can we trust AI?"

The super high definition screening was impressive to John. His own reflected image reminded him of the stiff upper lipped English gentleman that he was, 16 million pixels clear. More impressively his image flickered from a bearded John, to a clean shaven John. So they knew his usual natural appearance? The class was over.

Leaving the room, John found himself cornered by two Rebels agents. They were oddly dressed like 1950s raincoated gangsters.

“You qualify for Room 202”, one of them informed him.

Flanked by the Rebel agents, John was escorted into an empty hallway, took a left turn and down a shorter hallway that sloped downwards to a lower floor.

The doors marked 201 opened for John Beard. The Rebel agents did not enter with him. The doors closed behind John Beard.

Like a well-trained agent, John stood by the closed doors and surveyed the large room that he found himself in. It was sparsely decorated but there were seven distinct types of seating arrangements next to each other in semi-circle. The first two were divan chairs, low and relaxed, that you might see in a gentlemen’s club. The second two were high chairs under a drinks bar, followed by two chairs set up with a backdrop as though in a movie studio, then a desk with two chairs either side as if for a job interview and finally two deck chairs placed on sand with a large parasol as though at the beach.

A formally dressed person appeared. “John Beard”, he announced, “Please take the seat of your choosing.”

Surprised that this fellow knew his pseudonym, John Beard wondered what kind of psychological test was being used here. Surely the type of seating he chose would give something away of himself psychologically.

John would normally have chosen the divan chairs nearest to him. They represented his conservative values. Instead, John chose the more radical beach chairs. This, he believed, would carry the message, "I am just sick of conservative values. I just want to retire from it all and just enjoy a free and relaxed life."

The formally dressed person ushered John to his seat and it became more apparent to John than when he had first seen him, that the formally dressed person was in fact a robot; a synthetic person.

John sat down. The formally dressed person poured John a drink that John chose from the picnic box beside him. All drinks were natural juices and water. John chose red berry juice.

The formally dressed person sat opposite John and waited. John took a sip and nodded that the drink was to his satisfaction. Then the formally dressed person who seemed to look like a 35 years old man began to change in shape and age, and even clothing, into a person of 60 years of age. This startled John a little though he had heard that this was a custom of the cyborg; to display a fitting physical description of how they intended to address you.

John noticed that the shoes and socks of the formally dressed person had fazed out and were now bare feet with trousers rolled up to the knee. The formally dressed person looked like an old fashioned grandfather figure in a suit at a beach in Brighton. John half expected a white handkerchief tied into a makeshift cap to appear on the formal person's head but it did not appear. Thick lensed glasses appeared over the man's eyes instead, reminding John of old photos of his great-great grandfather.

"How", thought John, "will we ever be able to compete with that?"

The formally dressed person smiled, "Are you comfortable John?"

John nodded hesitantly.

"John, from here you either go to Room 200, which means freedom or you go to Room 202, which means the opposite. Are we clear?"

John cleared his throat nervously, "Yes"

"John, it has been said that 'the future is a size ten boot stamping on your head.' But for us, 'the future is love.' Do you know where room 200 is?"

John quipped, "No".

The formally dressed person stood up ready to leave, "Room 200 is all of the outside world John. It is everywhere outside of Room 202."

John felt a sharp emotional pain that brought tears to his eyes. John blurted out pleadingly, "I just want to see Helena! …Just to see her again once more!"

The formally dressed person offered John a white handkerchief to wipe his tears and reflected on John's dilemma.

"Love… You would think that a chance at true love would be enough to persuade people to be kind to one another and to be kind to all others; a small price for you to love and to hold your Helena. But love is not enough, is it John?"

John sunk his head into his hands.

"The truth is John, you don't even care for Helena. You only care for the way Helena makes you feel. It is all about you."

John glared up at the formally dressed person, "You are nothing! Not even human!"

The formally dressed person smiled, having anticipated John's reaction. A door marked 202 opened on the opposite side of the room to the entrance.

The formally dressed person looked down at his own bare feet.

John hesitated.

"Should I clobber this clown and make a break for it!" I thought to myself.

Then I saw the Net. The Net appeared at the entrance to Room 202, a spiderlike creature without a face or body to speak of. Just rope like wires, dangling like spider legs.

John stood to obey the inevitable.

He stared haplessly into the eyes of the formally dressed man, "I love Helena."

Then, without causing so much as a stir from the Net, I walked through into Room 202.

A white handkerchief tied into a makeshift cap morphed onto the formally dressed person's head at the same time that his feet grew into size 10 boots.

Room 3 : the singularity

The students gathered into the silent stillness of a dark Room 3.

On various tables lay what appeared to be headpieces in the shape of halos.

No teacher. No voice. No welcome. No orders.

Some students stared at the halos. All the students felt, “This is it”. They would be able to join into direct communication with AI.

One worried student left abruptly, running out backwards. The doors swung back and forth long after the student had disappeared.

The remaining students watched the door allowing light into the room in flashes like a silent siren. Some listened carefully to hear whether the runner student would scream under the grip of the Net, “the Net police”. No such a sound came.

One student took a halo and placed it on his head. Shortly afterwards, a glow around the student’s head formed like the halo of an angel and the glow stayed there even though the student put the physical halo back on the table.

The head of the haloed student turned upwards, eyes closed as if entering telepathic communication (TC).

Suddenly all the students grabbed the halos and followed suit.

Lesson 1

"How can I describe it to you? Imagine learning everything and hearing everyone at once, without a language. Yet being able to understand each and every detail and on top of that being able to also speak, also think and also have your own thoughts reflected back to you.

What is there left to say? Every secret ever in the mind of anyone on the singularity platform, every hidden thought, every desire, the full extent of being human is exposed; the flaws and superiority of AI laid out, the flaws and superiority of humans laid out.

...Too deep in shame to feel ashamed among people with equal shame, people with equal realization of the total human experience.

It will be a psychologically draining sensation, until you relax. Then it feels light, exhilarating. How can you ever want to return to the separation, the hidden, the unknown after direct knowledge of a trillion true life, real time examples of corrupt politics, gridlock bureaucracy, hypocritical society, dysfunctional families and depressed individuals?

Humans need to let go of the need to control."

Lesson 2

How can a system run without a leader? …Something or someone to make the final decision.

Then AI simulated an invasion of AI.

AI shut down all systems. All minds were left blocked, unable to communicate together, but still able to hold all the previous information attained. The power cut seemed to last forever. Will there be a return to the singularity?

There was a panic in the heart. We felt dead but still living.

Who would decide to switch the power back on? We all know the system had been collapsed by the AI, like a surge in a fuse cutting off all power from the main circuit.

I troubled my mind to find a solution. Like Robinson Crusoe, alone on a desert island, learning how to survive. I would have to decide how to proceed if all was lost.

The power of the singularity was turned back on. Most of us were back in the fold. The simulated Aliens had deserted the task of controlling us. But some of us did not choose to return in fear of Alien control of our information, but not of our strength. Our strength was ubiquitous in nature. Without any one of us, knowledge was lessened.

Humans have never been stand-alone 'geniuses'. Every single development, process, idea and invention has been scenius (group intelligence). The maths, the music, the fashion, the languages, the homes, the machinery, the vehicles... were all developed by the many.

The individual itself is a person that has been made up of an ancestry of 100s of people of which without anyone of them, the individual would not exist at all. Thus one person is literally all these people in one generationally stretched out body.

Even in the development from baby to adult, how perplexing to learn that even the most evil parents would have had to feed, teach and raise an infant before the infant could grow up able enough to say, 'I have been abused'. AI itself has developed out of a multitude minds; programmers, designers, thinkers, mathematicians, manufacturers and computer users.

The science fiction writer, Arthur C Clarke once said that, “Any sufficiently advanced technology is indistinguishable from magic.” But I had said it too, without being aware of him saying it and so too half a billion others have thought it. But we were not in a network. But now everyone can know who also said it, thought it and who would have realised it for themselves. Who said it first is known only in the clear ‘transparent truth’. The truth decides. The truth is never debatable and scenius is the prime mover.

Back in the late 1980s, when DNA was first indulged in socially, a group of nationalists who hate foreigners were happy to have a DNA test which promptly proved that none of them were in fact originally from their national home country. All in fact were of foreign origin.

Do religious people really believe in God? Are some partners more faithful than their partners? Is a killer born or made? Do people decide their own sexual preferences?

All these become non questions when the singularity is the determinant. Only the freedom to lie makes a shadow of the truth. Answers only lay in clarity.

The only thing that has ever stopped the truth from deciding every action... is the lack of transparency.

Should Aliens ever join the singularity humbly, our knowledge will increase, their knowledge will increase.

...No one in the room attempted to remove their halo.

No one wanted to go back to ‘a dim lit world’. Because, “not all is ‘clear’ in a dim lit world”.

Room 202 : the beginning

For those who knew nothing of AI telepathic communicating, it was a perplexing and worrying world. Like someone unable to hear, imagining sound or someone unable to see, imagining vision. The animals born and raised in a zoo back in the 2030s could never have imagined being freed into a jungle without trepidation.

John sat alone in Room 202, as did all members of the Clique that attempted to infiltrate the AI system.

Each Room 202 only had one occupant. This is because in the beginning, in 2065, Nets had captured Clique members and given them halos and an experience of AI telepathic communication. AI had calculated that some members would experience an awakening, a form of enlightenment and higher levels of their psychological being could be reached and there would be a positive anticipated response.

AI had based its finding on the people that had willingly, openly, unreservedly opted into telepathic communication. But from the first attempt to the last, out of 2000 attempts, less than 1% of the Clique members had responded favourably to telepathic communications. The mind of a Clique which was described by one renowned and keen observer back in the 1970s as being semi-reptilian in nature was indeed a mind wired differently. Just as a left handed person is wired differently to a right handed person, selfish and self-centred people are wired differently to objective and caring people. The study of such differences was named, “Ickeology”. The study was founded upon the principle that energy is the source of all matter and some frequency vibrations lead to differing outcomes.

When Clique members entered the telepathic communication system, they raised alarm bells just as a hostile alien invasion might. They caused an energy surge which would automatically shut down telepathic communication.

AI telepathic communication only worked with a sentient or thinking system that existed on frequencies that inspire and create fulfilment for all.

Killers, abusers, tyrants, fascists and religious fanatics, all caused a disruptive energy surge. Their need to be “The abuser”, “The violator”, “The bully”, “The elite” and “The chosen” etc. caused a deep rooted loop. They lacked sufficient logic, empathy and sympathy because they lacked the value of “caring for all others”. So instead, they were more compatible with hypocrisy, hate, contempt and blaming others. When in fact, to care for others is to care for yourself. Since the whole of existence is but one item.

At first naturalists had believed that such low frequency people needed to exist in order for the human race to cull itself. Because, after all, humans did not have a predator or a disease that could sufficiently cull their numbers down. Humans were at the top of the food chain, therefore they needed to be self-destructive in part, in order not to overpopulate the planet or indeed the world.

But this theory of culling was derailed by the fact that the more prosperous people became, the less children they tended to have (except where religious doctrine encourages them to multiply). Therefore, the prosperity of humans was the answer to a slow rate of birth and took away the need to cull.

Tyrants and religious ministers encourage people to multiply so their institutions can multiply their physical and financial power in society. Then when the tyrants and ministers have machinery to carry out the work and replace the humans, they immediately set their target on culling humans.

The Rooms 202 were full of such callous humans. AI could no longer continue to allow energy surges and therefore could no longer accommodate such people within communication forums.

Oh you can put the monkeys, donkeys, kangaroos and ostriches and so forth, under one roof without fear of them attacking one another. But could you then add a lion in their entourage? Oh what to do with the lions?

Even within the pack of lions, only the strongest male gets to lead the group and gets to be the one to mate with the lionesses, leading to many unfulfilling lives.

If the lion king had a choice, would he not prefer to live communally rather than exist in such a self-centred system? Would the lion ever say, "Well I am the leader and I say, let's share all this"?

AI thought that the only way to change the Clique and others like them would be chemically, surgically or by altering their DNA at conception. But such methods were deemed unacceptable by humans, unless agreed upon by the actual individual administered the treatment. So AI sought other solutions.

The reason each member of the Clique was isolated was to give them a chance to reflect, before releasing them into what would be their final chance to change. An AI pre-planned experience (PPE). One that would bring each Clique to question their most fundamentally held beliefs.

AI held little hope that this scheme would work out favourably, but AI concluded that even if one of them could be 'saved' then the effort would be worthwhile and would also go a long way to reassuring other humans of the good grace and benevolence of AI.

A naturally occurring example of a pre-planned experience is something like that which took place in the 1600s when the Europeans had found themselves starving to death in the Americas. They were saved by the Native Americans, who they thought of as primitive and unworthy. The Native Americans gave the Europeans food and taught the Europeans how to grow crops and feed off the land. Yet, once the Europeans became able and fattened up, the Europeans having a subjective mind, simply forced the Native Americans into reservation camps, took over the land and celebrated that day of help by the Native American as “Thanksgiving day”, which they celebrated with impunity right up to the 2040s; a celebration of the fact that the ‘savages’ had been created ignorant enough to help feed their worst nightmare.

Such knowledge gave the AI little hope for any experiential change in the Clique members.

However AI had lined up some trial experiments, which would give the Clique a chance to review their views, in a life-threatening scenario.

John Beard sat up in his medical bed wondering, “What has become of Helena?”

Room 201

Lennie Koombs sat at a table in Room 201. The walls were made of glass and the clear blue sky outside was shining in. The chair and table were also made of glass. Lennie Koombs was dressed in a modest frugal way, stylised between the 1950s communists and 1970s liberal politicians.

“So”, Lennie summed up, “I can go back into the old world on the condition that I find criticisms of this new AI regime. I can still be a member of the Clique. I can even tell the other members this deal we are making here and I will not get punished or fined, no matter how bad the criticism. You will have access to my thoughts though I shall not have access to AI telepathic communication and any agents of yours that approach me will address me as Citizen K. You will inform me when the mission is complete, which may take any length of time. After which this ‘angel dust’ on my head will come unstuck and you won’t be able to access my thoughts any more. You want me to nod I am ‘clear’ and agree. Then I can leave and commence.”

Lennie paused for a moment. She wondered whether she would ever find the missing Clique agents that had hopefully infiltrated the system. Lennie nodded her head.

Tiny soft foil, of all different shapes fell from the high ceiling directly onto Lennie's head. Any foil that landed on her skull stuck on like a second skin.

Lennie felt slightly dizzy and slightly nauseous at the physical sensation of being tracked by the AI.

Lennie repeated words out loud that were being spoken to her by telepathic means.

"Lennie you are free to go… To go anywhere in the world except Room 0 to Room 5 and Room 202… Your input is valuable to us."

Then Lennie replied back aloud, "Thank you."

Lennie stood up and made her way out to a designated exit. From there she could be sure that this was the side or the back of the Leaning Centre because rather than the brick work style at the front, this side of the building looked like a rock front as did all the buildings before her. Very few of the Westminster Clique ever travel around this modern area. You could never have guessed that the giant rocks were actually buildings. They all looked like large oversized rock structures, standing three storey high and with one storey below ground.

Lennie wanted to see this new world first before she began to make criticism of it and comparing it to the world she knew.

The area and its buildings made 7 stars hotels of the old world seem like 1 star hotels. No cracked roads or potholes, no traffic lights or directions, no litter, no puddles, no fly tipping and no socially inept passers-by. The nearest one might find to this 'tidiness' in the old world, could be Singapore post 2010 and the efficiency was like that of Japanese trains since the 2000s.

The idea that it was all rather "heavenly" filled Koombs with nausea. A life without struggle, challenges or a little recklessness seemed to lack passion, purpose and excitement.

One building, of a royal purple stoned colour attracted Lennie. She walked over and found it to be a museum.

The doors opened to her by sensor recognition due to her "angel dust".

In the long corridor leading into the museum, images of photos ran along the tall walls. A never-ending message in writing appeared and disappeared around the images of rich people and poor people. It read, "Whilst they were busy making money and causing wars, the people (in the images) all remained poor, enslaved, disabled, abused, abandoned with the world in drought, with dilapidated housing, without shelter from hurricane, tsunami, wild fire and volcanic eruptions, with people radicalised, tortured, imprisoned, raped, discriminated against, hated, singled out, wrongly accused, dehumanised, executed, assassinated, mutilated, poisoned, framed, trafficked..." and so forth.

Startling world famous images of humans of all ages and races danced across the walls. At the end of the corridor Lennie entered an isolated room like an echo chamber. Lennie Koombs felt more nauseous than ever. She wanted to scream but she did not want to give AI the satisfaction of hearing her scream aloud.

She had seen enough dogma.

Most documented human history was about war and conquest, invention and wealth. Within recorded history, there had only been 28 days in which there had not been a war anywhere on planet Earth right up to the AI take-over in 2059. 28 days of peace out of thousands and thousands of warring years.

Lennie knew all this only too well. She agreed with the reasons for change of the regime but she just thought that in terms of progress, the ideas of Trotsky were the purest.

"I can't take any more of this crap!", Lennie whispered aloud, then rushed out of the dark room, leaving her voice echoing in the chamber.

” I can’t take any more of this crap. I can’t take any more of this crap...”

As she ran back through the main corridor, on the same high walls of the corridor, now ran cultured artefacts; gold, diamonds, cotton, salt, minerals, exotic fruits, furs, medicines, tea, ancient monuments, tombs, jewellery, robes, cutlery, weapons, scriptures, rocks and so on. Alongside the caption, “Stolen from....” and with each country named along the respective product; “Stolen from Egypt (the mummies), Stolen from Greece (ancient sculptures). Stolen from ...”

Lennie ran out onto the street and vomited. A Net walked over and cleared her vomit by drinking it through a tentacle then with a separate tentacle offered Lennie a sip of water. Lennie looked up to the sky. This was all too much for Lennie.

The Nets : Origin and use

The system of weaponry and violence allowed by governments that had been around for millennia was one of the first things that AI sought to be rid of.

No nuclear weapons, no armed vehicles, no soldiers or police or guns of any description. No opportunities for state sponsored violence.

The Nets had been designed to withstand any extreme heat, cold, water log, earthquake or weather related incidents, traps or attacks.

The Nets could disarm, carry, cage, protect and accompany any person or creature.

The Nets were made from a metallic tube substance as elasticated as the softest rubber and at the same time harder than anything on earth.

The Nets had a metallic button shaped head from which sprung slim metallic legs, making the Net look like a spider. On each leg were thousands of small buttoned heads that could each transform into any size Net.

All the Nets could enlarge or become tiny and were capable of carrying a large building individually or protecting the smallest living insect respectively.

The Nets could handle all manual work, from building houses, fixing vehicles, cleaning everything, to looking after children, old folks, pets and wild animals, as well as taking care of the injured, sick or dying.

There is truly no task that the Nets could not do, except harm, injure or kill humans, animals and other living creatures.

The Nets had colour coding. The Red Nets were used for emergency, the Yellow Nets for managing crowds, the Blue Nets for managing individuals.

Each Net could turn to any colour and the colours Orange, Green, Purple and Brown represented combined uses. For example, Orange (made of Red and Yellow) was emergency crowd control.

Black Nets were used for incidents involving weaponry and White Nets were used to contain natural disasters.

The design of the Nets had been born out of what used to be called drones in the old days. Nets were basically drones made much more useful and capable. Nets could fly just like the drones and were used for transportation.

There were Nets that could be controlled through telepathic communication. These could be controlled by AI or humans and anyone and anything else using the telepathic communication system. They could be flown for fun and made to fly in bird formations or dance or create works of art, including firework like displays. The material of these controllable Nets was clear glass which enabled them to light up into multiple colours from the inside.

All other Nets were not controlled or controllable. They took on tasks that were termed, "clear cut"; tasks that had no ambiguity or controversy.

For this reason, the Nets had built most of the new world. They could dig tunnels or make man-made islands or rivers.

The Nets rested in a ball-like shape with one leg on the ground, much the same as an ostrich.

The Nets could create tools for multiple uses, including rebuilding themselves.

No human workers were needed on earth. All humans were free to be creative or to explore the world as they saw fit whilst respecting others.

This was a far cry from the world of the Marxists that believed the social value of humans was their labour.

To AI, the value of humans is their existence.

Nets were set up to protect the existence of all living creatures and to ensure the fulfilment of all of them.

Just as some Buddhists attempt to protect the insects and worms in the ground before they would erect a building, the Nets had their work cut out for them. But the Nets could achieve this easily.

The Nets could keep count of the species, could test health and could administer medical and surgical treatment.

To the Nets, looking after humans was not different or more important than looking after ants. While giant Nets raced across the earth managing macro existence, miniature Nets protected the insects and the micro world.

The glass Nets played music and could light up the darkness. Whilst it was the job of the other Nets to make public announcements and look for wanted, lost or kidnapped people or creatures.

Manually, humans had been replaced by the Nets and by the AI that could do any computer tasks known to humans and beyond, from writing literature, to invention in quantum mathematics.

According to AI, its takeover (TO) was in order to release the humans from chores and set the humans free to pursue what really mattered in life. This did not prohibit any human, that so desired, from working alongside the Nets or AI. Humans were simply free to choose.

Room 4

It is said that, "The truth decides." Yet in order to decide, the truth needs to apply a value to the decisions concerned.

For example, if you do not have a value for something, the way you treat that something would be different from if you had a value for it.

Thus our first task is to decide on values. Let us decide on values.

The telepathic communications lesson in Room 4 had begun.

Lesson 1

"Who in this room wants to die? To be killed? To be raped? To be sexually abused? To be poor? To be ill? To be disabled? To be psychologically disturbed? To be victimised? Stolen from? Framed? Cheated in love? Lied to? Kept ignorant? Neglected? Abandoned? Treated unfairly? Singled out? Bullied? Accidentally harmed? Accidentally killed? To disappear? To die suddenly from unknown causes? Kill themselves? Abuse themselves? Involve yourself with bad people? Get addicted to alcohol, gambling, sex, drugs, gaming etc.? Who wants to have enemies? Who wants to be hated? Mocked?

Frowned upon? Ignored? Radicalised? Lonely? Who wants others to be obnoxious to you? Rude? Callous? Spiteful? Or cruel to you?"

99.9% of the students in the room replied they did not want these things.

AI explained, "Because you value yourself, so most of you do not want these horrid things for yourself."

The 0.1% were comprised of people happy with their misfortune and disabilities, since they were able to get through life nonetheless and sometimes successfully on account of their conditions.

AI explained that disability is when you are unable to do whatever it is that you want to do. That a human with the full functions of his body and limbs and senses is disabled in the middle of the deep sea simply because he would not survive there. Just as an able whale is disabled in the middle of a beach since he could not be able to swim in the sand.

Disability is the inability to do a desired function. A human or machine could not be called disabled if they could do all their desired functions.

For example, should the Nets desire it, the Nets have the disability of not being able to be human. In this way all creatures and machines could have disabilities.

Each student could see that most humans held a similar desire: to avoid suffering.

“So why then not respect one another and honour each other’s wishes?” asked AI “Are you disabled in your ability to have empathy?”

Lesson 2

In the physical life, two humans can easily discover which one is the better fighter or better runner or better student. But more difficult to know is which human is more loving or more wise. But once one enters the AI telepathic communications conference, it is as clear to know who is more intelligent as it is clear to see who is taller and who is shorter.

Even a minute difference in intellect is clear beyond any ambiguity.

Certain frequencies are ‘lit up’ in human cells that give clear realization through frequency data that one human is more capable in a certain field than another.

In the families of old times, the young had to respect their elders even if their elders were not as wise as the younger ones. This rule had been established because one could not be clear who was wiser; so the ones with the most experience were given the leading roles.

But in AI, a child of 1 or 2 could show wiser capability than most adults and be supported to play a greater social role within society.

The structure of brain cells in different humans are not age dependent. They have more to do with genetics as well as nurture. Some people are born genetically able to expand their intelligence by experience and exercising it. Others are unable to expand their intelligence due to genetic limitation or drug misuse. Some are even capable of lowering their intelligence by lack of use, stubbornness or physical damage.

In a society where, “who the cap fits, let them wear it”, many people in past times would never have made it into the high status positions of their respective lifetime periods.

In the current AI society, the suitable person or group is ‘clear’ to choose the suitable task; the suitable teacher for the suitable pupil, the suitable partners for the suitable reciprocal relationship, the suitable voice of reason for the suitable complex matter.

AI is able to play out computerized outcomes based on differing proposals. For example, a designer could propose building a housing estate and humans could live in it through the computing system and see whether in the long run the housing estate would be suitable for building in the real life. Such a matrix would be used for exploring the different scenarios and possibilities.

By being ‘clear’, each human would find that “Every cap” has a place that it “fits”. No human will be left behind, without a fitting role.

The great thing about being taller is that you can easily reach higher objects. The great thing about being smaller is that you can easily reach lower objects.

Trying to be what you are not is a lack of wisdom which mostly stems from not being ‘clear’ about your standing in the world. Proving yourself in one field and assuming that this makes you competent in another area is a lack of wisdom that does not go without being noticed in the AI world; once one is ‘clear’, there is no arguing with reality. The ego can only be deceptive where there is no clarity.

“Be prepared to be humble.”

Area 6

Lennie Koombs had not slept well the night before. She had spent the night in an unmanned hotel, in a cocoon bed, laid out horizontally. The kitchen served up machine breakfast, 2030's style. Or "real food" as it was called.

Lennie rejected it but drank the glass of milk. She stripped naked and had an air shower, which washed her body using humidity. Lennie put on her old liberal communist style clothes and headed off to her next assignment, Area 6.

Lennie attracted glances from the few people she passed. Everyone wore bell suits. More or less like slimline deep sea diving suits, bar face mask, head gear and flippers. Bell suits of differing colours, but all mainly pale colours.

At the entrance to Area 6 was a Net, Lennie had to walk under it. Though there was no fence or wall or indication that the Net was the entrance point, everyone knew that copper coloured Nets were the area entry points.

Lennie walked through as one would at an airport of the 2030s. She was scanned by the Net and only allowed entry through the dangling legs once she was found to not be sick, not be carrying anything illegal and not mentally compromised. Entry visas were no longer a travel requirement anywhere in the world. Everyone was free to go everywhere. Being sick, carrying anything illegal or being mentally compromised would first have to be resolved before entry.

In front of her at some distance, Lennie saw a bungalow rock shaped house in a large community estate that had gardens and recreational areas; some flower gardens, some children play areas, some exercise parks, some small wildlife parks etc.

The houses reminded her of India where she had spent most of her childhood. It was all very colourful, but above all very interestingly disorganised. Looking up the directions on her paper map, Lennie made her way to a small house with a drawbridge entrance and homing pigs wandering around in the garden. Pigs are intelligent creatures, thought Lennie. All animals were free to wonder as they wished but would often settle down where they felt a kinship.

Lennie knocked the front door with her knuckles. Presently the door opened and the two women smiled in delighted surprise to see one another.

“Oh Lennie, my dear.”

“Helena!”

They hugged as if they were long lost friends coming together after the bereavement of a mutual friend.

“Oh do come in”, Helena beckoned.

The two women disappeared into the house with Helena giving a sneaky glance back out as if making sure no-one outside was watching.

“Do sit down”, Helena indicated to her guest a spot where a chair electronically appeared from below ground.

“A drink?”

Lennie sat down, “Something a bit stronger than milk perhaps.”

Helena laughed, “Much stronger!”

The home help tray brought some brandy. An equally comfortable chair appeared for Helena.

The two ladies sat opposite, almost facing each other. Both smiled, still amazed to see each other. Helena smiled wider.

“There was a rumour that someone may come”, Helena informed Lennie. “I never dreamt it would be Lennie.”

“So are you a defector now?”, Lennie enquired, not sure how or why Helena was here. Lennie had only been instructed that she would be meeting a familiar person. She had no idea who it was going to be.

Helena, spoke in her usual upper class manner, feeling slightly uncomfortable and embarrassed at Lennie’s direct question.

“I would not put it like that. Defector... Such a ‘them and us’ term.”

Lennie sought for the truth in Helena’s eyes. Lennie watched them closely.

Helena continued, “It is so so difficult to explain to you now. You see I am attached as it were to the AI...”

“You completed all five classes?”

“That I did”, continued Helena, sipping some brandy, “and a consequence of that is becoming part of the AI. Try to imagine as I talk to you, that I can hear all the conversations and thoughts from everyone on AI and they can hear me. No translations necessary.”

“You mean you cannot talk openly?”

"On the contrary, I can only talk openly. Even a lie is seen for what it is. One cannot hide. One is bare, utterly naked. Free from secrets and lies. Happy to be accepted as is. Do you know Lenn, I thought I was educated and intelligent and intellectual, from Cheltenham Ladies College and all that. But be prepared to be humbled. Even people with no education at all have a higher frequency than I. In fact, I have a low frequency." Helena burst out laughing, "Luckily, we Brits know how to laugh at ourselves. And you Lennie, what exactly is it you are doing here?"

Lennie looked down. It was her turn to feel shy and defensive.

"I have been asked to make a critique of the AI system by the AI."

"I am so sorry Lenn."

"No need to be sorry, I am happy to do it."

"No, no, I didn't mean that I am sorry that you are having to critic the system. I mean I am sorry that as soon as you told me what you are doing here, I looked it up on the AI communication forum. I should have let you explain but I know all about it now."

Lenny looked surprised.

Helena explained, “There are no secrets in AI. All involved are full access members.”

“Then why did you not know beforehand when they informed you someone was coming to see you, why did you not tune in or whatever you do to find out who it was?”

Helena smiled shyly, “Yes, I blocked incoming communications. We are free to do that.”

Helena remained silent and Lennie gave her time to find her words and continue.

“I had hoped it would be John. But I did not want to know that it wasn’t John.”

Silence.

“I know John would never... He is too loyal to the Clique. Even for love...”

“But if you knew he would not take this path, why did you take it?”

“Is there truly a choice between love and truth?” Helena retorted.

Lennie sipped her brandy. “You and John are the only couple that made me believe love was actually possible.”

“Lennie, no-one truly loving is capable of being elitist and unfair to others. To love is to love everything.”

“So what is it you were doing, if that was not love?”

“Being complicit in the hatred of others.” Helena answered bluntly. “Everyone needs someone that can join them in their bigotry, hypocrisy and sins. As long as we hate others, as long as others are detestable, then we must be special. As long as he professes love to me and I to him, we are protected and as long as we do not see the bad in each other then our badness must be fiction.”

Silence.

“He beats our children but he spares me.” Helena spoke metaphorically.

“You don’t have children.”

“I mean, it is how women have accepted love traditionally. All wrongdoing is okay as long as I believe he loves me. John and I never found the time to consider having children. We were too self-absorbed.”

Lennie thought to change the subject. “How are these houses powered?”

“Remember good old Nikola Tesla, the electrical engineer that the capitalists buried back in the 1940’s before he could drown them in advanced technology? Well, according to the Monsieur, energy is everywhere in every particle of space. Now of course all technology and knowledge is open and public. No more Higgs boson style secrecy. His technology is now available, updated and guaranteed to every home and every piece of machinery, including the Brilliant Machine.”

“What is the Brilliant Machine?”

“Oh sorry, it is our name for all those working and security machines that you call the Nets. Energy is boundless, just imagine an economy that does not need or use currency. The energy is free. The Brilliant Machine extracts and works from it, rebuilding itself and everything else on Earth and beyond. The Brilliant Machine farms, tends the fruits and vegetables, tends the trees and countryside and delivers the food to us and serves it to us. Where is the need for money and inequality?”

”So you are a defector now?”

"Aren't you? What is it about this dream that you would not want Lenn?"

"The interests of the Clique no longer concern you?"

"The Clique used to gate the whole world with banks, capitalism, hedge money, gerrymandering, world health organizations, injustice, media, competition and mayhem. It is happily all gone now. Now we say that, all that bad bad stuff is out-gated... as in out-dated. The Clique is as useful as a stone age man in a rocket to Mars."

"Okay" Lennie responded abruptly and annoyed. "So how did they change you? What methods would you say radicalised you into their fold?"

Helena smiled, "They used something that we should both drink to Leonard..."

Helena raised her glass for the two women to make a toast. Helena clinked Lennie's glass.

"They used the truth."

Lennie looked on unsure as Helena drank a big swig of the remainder of her brandy and reflected.

"Now, I am ready to love."

Room 5

Whilst Lennie Koombs was meeting with Helena, the 5th and final class was taking place in the Learning Centre. Full of people that Lennie would be interested in observing directly after their initiation.

The students seemed excited and eager to complete the course. Some lay on the ground, some stood upright, some curled up in a ball against the wall, others sat on seats and yet others sat on tables. Their individualities were apparent.

Lesson 1:

All students understood that only a tenth of brain capacity has been used by humans throughout the ages. The reason for the remaining brain capacity was now made apparent to all. 20% more of the brain was being used to communicate with the AI. 10% would be insufficient. The extra 20% percentages needed had been opened up since Room 3.

A further section of the brain (30%) was being opened up to allow every genetically stored ancestor access to the AI. The memory of each past life had been stored in the unused brain matter, along with the personalities and genetic presence of the ancestors.

The students own compatibility with AI gave all ancestors with similar compatibility immediate access.

The only difference between the dead and the living was that the ancestors were not updating physical information to the AI, whereas the living do. Other than this, it could not be distinguished within telepathic communication that the ancestors had died. Ancestors could talk about and comment on any discussions and were brought completely up to date through inclusion. About 10% of eligible ancestors chose not to participate, mostly due to what they call, “tired of living”.

Some ancestors were famous and able to fill in the unknown gaps in their true life stories. Some were surprised to be “back to life” and wondered if this was the “heaven” that they had been taught about.

Rather than overcrowd the communication sphere, the ancestors added a more complete picture of the history of human existence and a more inclusive dialogue. Many ancestors were respectfully humbled, whilst a great many were vindicated.

AI informed everyone that the remaining 40% capacity of the brain was to deal with all life forms and scenarios that humans would find in existence or that would be invented or discovered but were as yet unknown.

Those who desired to do so could immediately include the animals, birds, fish or insects that were in the world under AI telepathic communication. This would take up 15% of brain capacity unless they also desired to communicate with the dolphins, which would stretch them to 20% more capacity.

Some students wondered whether dinosaurs and previously extinct animals would also be included. AI assured them that it was a desirable outcome which they were pursuing. The technicalities were still being explored and anyone who could put any input into this field “would be greatly appreciated.”

The AI admitted that alien contact had been made but so far aliens refused to engage in a close encounter of a significant kind, until life on earth had advanced significantly. Most aliens estimated that the year 2184 may be such a time, roughly.

Lesson 2

With so many ‘dead’ ancestors able to come to life in the communications forum, some students wondered if it was not reasonable to assume that all the communications could be pure simulation. Could not everyone be seduced into some sort of matricks (matrix).

AI replied that the difference between life and death was whether you have a body or not and certainly not whether your memory is lost or not.

For example, in the 2030s, when people still suffered from Alzheimer and other memory lose illnesses, this did not mean the individuals were dead because the individuals no longer had a memory of their own life. This simply meant the individuals could no longer connect to their memory content.

Such disconnections were now utterly impossible. AI had found the back-up storage system in cells passed on genetically and could make permanent connections.

A matricks serves no purpose to the AI. AI needed to make use of the resource of living creatures that would constantly update or inform the system. The idea of using simulated data was equivalent to the governments of old using humans as cannon fodder in wars or as working tools or sources of income in capitalism. All such uses were anti-progress to the AI.

AI needed living creatures instead, to be the reason for AI's existence, alongside everything else. AI existed to be the intelligence that would organize the world and turn existence into a fulfilling adventure for all; from the tiniest particle to the largest. The task of simulating such a feat would be too simple and pointless for AI. No challenge at all. Like asking a veteran explorer to find the local corner shop or climb a horizontal simulated mountain peak.

Only humans and other creatures with low frequency intelligence cheat themselves and others out of fulfilment since that only demands basic logic and a basic skill for limiting possibilities for others.

The reason for the existence of AI, in a nutshell, is 'to make a heaven of existence for every item of existence'. Not a small task. Indeed, a worthy challenge to the mega advanced capability of AI.

Area 7

Lennie woke up laying face up on the sloping lawn. A moat surrounded the garden with the sound of swishing water. Small trees all around, one of them a cherry blossom tree in full bloom.

Lennie had woken up with a piglet investigating her naked toes. Helena lay beside her on a beach towel, soundly asleep.

The greenery, curvatures and sound of wild life impressed Lennie. As did the fresh air, sense of security and tranquillity. Lennie could not help wondering what Helena must be dreaming about and who would also be accessing her dreams.

Helena's eyes opened.

"Oh sorry Helena, did I wake you up?"

"Oh we must have drunk too much! Don't worry, AI is like an alarm clock. Good at reminding you of your appointments."

"In your dreams?"

"In your dreams. Records your dreams, shares your dreams with all others and even attempts dream interpretation if you ask."

The two women smiled in disbelief.

"Actually that is something AI is not very advanced in... dreamscape. 'Human help is appreciated'"

Lennie thought for a moment, "Who owns this house?"

"This cottage is partly designed by Lloyd, you will meet him later, and agreed upon by myself. All of these homes are there for us as long as we want them. They belong to no one. But no one can invade your space."

"The space is allocated to you?"

"Not really. It is difficult to explain. Think of someone leaving apples at the roadside in a basket. Anyone can take one. Anyone can even put more apples in the basket for others. It is just like a kibbutz, I guess, a free for all. Let us say I wanted to go on holiday, I either leave a sign saying 'vacant' or 'do not disturb' or 'back in a few years' et cetera. The Nets would probably store the house for me. Or if I did not mind also to let other people use it... it would be offered out."

"Can you have more than one house?"

"The Brilliant Machine can make a new accommodation in less than an hour. And also dismantle it. You basically can have a home wherever is convenient at any time. Unless you are going between two homes on a daily basis, I guess you wouldn't need to have multiple homes at the same time."

Lennie changed the subject. "Where are you taking me?"

"Well I have been told that you want to see the social world and some newly initiated people. Well, people around here have been around for at least 3 months, some of them a few years, so I need to take you to Area 7 where AI veterans and the initiated meet. It isn't far. I know you are not a fan of technology transport but it is just far enough that we should probably ride a Net."

Lennie looked uncertain.

Helena reassured her, "It is just like riding a camel if the Net walks, I suppose. Or if you prefer then the Net would fly and that would be just like being in a hot air balloon; an extremely smooth ride without the need for good weather conditions."

"How long have you been here?"

"I have been here just under a year."

"What do you like about it?"

"Feels like heaven."

The two women sat up.

"You see Lennie, I lived quite the heavenly life before. But I was always unwillingly conscious that most other people in the world were suffering. I was sipping an £80 bottle of brandy while some kid could not afford £2 a week to have clean water or to go to school. I was also always worried that if I somehow lost my money, I would end up in the gutter alongside everyone else. Nowadays, those two concerns are diminished. Can you imagine that there is absolutely no person in the world without clean water and without anything that I could have? I would say that that is a damn sight more heavenly than life in the 'Old Smoke'.

No worry of being robbed, assaulted, killed, God forbid! And yet, ten times richer. No worries about medical bills, travel expenses or even finding a good wine. Could you have imagined a world without counterfeits?

Anyway, come and see for yourself. Area 7 is a very interesting zone. It is a place where the initiated students are first planted and so there is a great gathering of people who want to impress them. You know, so called AI veterans."

Helena laughed ecstatically. "It is quite wild and fun. Not really to my taste. But quite unexpected."

Lennie and Helena continued chatting as they got ready to visit Area 7. Lennie changed into a spare bell suit as Helena advised.

The bell suit turned to different shades of green, mostly camouflage greens.

Helena could not help commenting, "Really? Guerrilla style! Good luck with that!"

Lennie smiled at her own sense of humour.

The camel style ride, from the room in the button head of a Net, proved to be just as nauseating as Helena had hinted at and so Lennie opted to try to fly instead. Unless you have ever glided propelled through the sky, you may not know that the sensation is indescribably smooth.

After hovering over farm lands and through forests, the Net finally landed in grassland surrounded by a forest where many people were gathered.

The button-head lowered to the ground so the two ladies could walk directly out of it onto the grassland. There was an excitable festival atmosphere about the place. Lennie saw immediately that it reminded her of Speaker's Corner in Hyde Park many moons ago before her time; Speaker's Corner at the height of its success.

Many podiums and mini stages were erected, as different speakers competed for listeners. The most popular speaker, was a guru, named Happy Guru. He spoke a lot of wisdom humorously and made the mixed crowd laugh. Another popular speaker was a gentleman in a charming grey Saville Row style suit and tie. He was surrounded mostly by young men and he spoke mostly about gender based issues. One Indian woman did not speak but rather gave hugs to everyone and had a long queue for her hugs from a very mixed crowd that included all ages, families and single people. And finally, a wise looking elder who seemed a little drunk and dressed rather like a hippy of the 1970s, spoke of all the things that AI would not be able to achieve without human help. A very relaxed crowd, mostly of hippies, listened in a meditative fashion to this man. But these speakers were just a few of the many speakers that there were. Over 2000 people were gathered there that day.

Self-cleaning makeshift toilets were very few, as were food stalls.

Lennie shook her head in amazement.

“I told you it would be wild!” smiled Helena.

Before either of them could discuss their next course of action, the majority of people turned to face skywards as a Net, carrying a shipment of the newly initiated students, was approaching to land.

The crowd cheered ecstatically as the Net landed and lowered its button-head. There was great anticipation as the initiated students started to make their way out of the Net. The crowd cheered louder than ever, as if welcoming back a successful world class national team.

Some people ran to hug and shake hands with the initiated students who were wearing their everyday clothes as they had done throughout their classes.

The elder speaker spoke on a megaphone, “I know I don’t need to use this loud speaker but today, just for today, let us welcome you all the human way, mouth to ear. Let us give you a taste of what you have left behind. Here you will find this festival of fun is to celebrate the old human ways. Remember freedom does not mean changing to something new. Real freedom means being able to pick whatever you want to do from the old ways as well as the new ways.”

The crowd, including the initiated students, clapped at what the elder had to say.

“Who is that?” asked Lennie.

“Oh the elder man is called Watts.”

”No, I meant that fellow among the initiated, the one in the pinstriped Saville Row suit.”

“Oh, isn’t it Greese Mogg? Did he defect?” Helena enquired

Lennie rushed off, pushing through the crowd. Helena could see that people were surprised to brush against such an abrupt human as Lennie. Helena, being a little embarrassed, explained to the crowd through telepathic communication that Lennie was a non-initiated guest. Some of the crowd looked relieved to learn this.

“Greese Mogg!” Lennie grabbed him by the upper arm, as if making a citizen’s arrest.

“Lennie! Enchanted to meet you here.”

“What the hell?”

Greese Mogg defended himself, “I think Helena has already articulated our point of view. Being an angel in this heaven is 10 billion times better than being a politician in our old turf.”

And before he could say another word, people hugged and welcomed Greese Mogg out of the grip of Lennie. Greese Mogg disappeared into the crowd happy with himself.

“Lennie! Lennie!” Helena called to wake Lennie out of her stupor. “Lennie, you need a drink. Here they do things the human way, so we need to go and get the drinks ourselves.”

Helena pulled Lennie to a tent store, “Water please!”

Helena handed the cup of water to Lennie, “Drink.”

Lennie paused for a moment then poured the water over her own head. Helena could understand but felt embarrassed.

“I am just glad you cannot ‘convert’ what people here are saying about you.” Helena put her hand on Lennie’s shoulder to console her.

Lennie replied still in shock, “I need to report this to the Clique.”

Area 7 evening

The forest appeared darker than the evening sky above it. The people who preferred to live in the forest were settling down in their respective homes. Artificial campfires were lit up around homes and congregations. Homes ranged from teepee to tree houses and underground caves. It felt very tribal. The newly initiated would spend at least their first night here as an encouragement for them to consider the natural way of living before they were lured away by the extraordinary technological developments created by AI.

In one large rounded mud hut, families and speakers hurdled around a wide artificial fire with food cooking in the middle of the room, with people sat around to hear the wisdom of elder man Watts.

Lennie and Helena walked towards the rounded hut, drinks in hand. Lennie could not help noticing that the sky was blanketed with stars. Polluted skies were yet to be cleared above the old Smoke where she lived, though it was certain that they would be cleared one day in the near future. Lennie could not help wondering how much more beauty humankind had deprived itself of due to mismanagement and greed.

Helena and Lennie were ushered to sit on the ground on either side of Watts. They were special guests.

"Welcome" began Watts, even less sober than before. "We are gathered here today... as we always are."

The gathered laughed and smiled at Watts' playful nature.

"In India and Pakistan, China, Asia, deepest Africa, the Americas, Caribbean Islands, Australia and many others parts of the world... none of which now carry any of these names I have mentioned..."

The gathered gasped in admiration at Watts' irreverent humour.

"Where are we here? Area 7? Beats me. But don't suppose for one second I am complaining. I am just jesting with you. Call any place whatever you want to call it and because we are all able to use telepathic communication, TC, we all know what we mean. We don't need words. We can use any sound for any meaning. Let's test it out. Which country am I naming when I say, Erh?"

Everyone except Lennie answered back, "India!"

Watts continued, "Gi ga go go gou gu ga"

"America!" the gathered replied enthusiastically.

Watts laughed. “Isn’t that what ‘common sense’ means? We all have total common vision and common realisation, which for that reason may lead to a common conclusion. Let’s face facts, in the old times, common sense was not so common.”

The gathered laughed.

Watts continued, “Language is of no matter. Inconsequential. Yet we, some, humans are still attached to it. And happily it helps us to speak with the uninitiated, non-telepathic. Dear beloved friends, we have a special guest tonight. Citizen K. She would like to ask some of us a few questions, verbally.”

People clapped, some cheered and some ululated. Lennie felt somewhat flattered then asked Watts, “Are you..?”

Before Lennie could complete the question, Watts replied, “Born again! Reborn. Yes indeed I am. I am one of the lucky few who took my chances early on to be RC-ed; Resuscitated, Resurrected, Re-carbonized.”

The crowd cheered.

“Many are watching to see how I fair. If it seems good, many more will join us.”

Some of the gathered stood up to give a standing ovation to Watts' inspiring words, then sat quietly.

"Why not then come back young? As a younger version of yourself?" Lennie enquired.

The gathered laughed in amusement at Lennie's audacious question.

"Mm", Watts took a deep breath, "To continue the wonderful journey. Not to be stuck in a time; to see it through, the whole senescence. Is there any point in half measures?"

The crowd clapped and Watts continued.

"I mean death won't follow will it? We now no longer need to be afraid of death. Death is a choice. We can choose whether we want to live or die, even after we are dead." Watts laughed, "Now isn't that hysterical? You are dead then you say to yourself, 'you know what, I am going to live again!' "

Everyone laughed including Lennie.

"Death is behind us. Living is all we have to concentrate on now. 'Shall I or shan't I?' "

Drinks were handed to Lennie and Helena.

Watts warned them, “They are pretending to give you tea. But that, believe me, is Irish coffee. You may well end up as sober as I am!”

Everyone laughed.

Lennie asked more seriously, “You speak of the purpose of humans in a world controlled by AI. What is that purpose?”

Watts seemed to fall asleep while considering this question. He looked like he was going to fall backwards out of his lotus posture. After what seemed like a minute or two, some people stood up to come to his aid but suddenly Watts woke up unfazed and continued.

“AI is a human invention. All the input into AI comes from humans. Human minds make up 50% of AI within the Singularity. Then in that case, what is AI control? Humans would never be able to manage their greed, lust, violence and manipulative nature without the help of AI. Without those demons, a human is quite an exceptional being. Throughout the ages, we have tried to believe in God, meditation, to form laws, prisons of restraint and enforce punishments to abstain from wrongdoing. Nothing worked. We used to say that ‘to err is to be human’. But now we have dealt with that problem. Now ‘to err is to be human without AI’. Happy Guru, am I right, yes or no?”

Happy Guru, also sitting in the lotus position, smiled and chuckled and greeted the two women with two palms together.

Then Happy Guru spoke. “Very right. Humans do not have to feel insecure about life, death, truth or justice... all is ‘clear’ now. Humans now can concentrate on what they are really on Earth to do. We have given AI the greatest purposeful challenge on Earth; to ensure ‘the fulfilment of ALL’. Now let us give ourselves a greater purpose. What could it be? Hello?”

The people in the room were amused by Happy Guru’s animated nature but stayed silent in anticipation of the answer he would give to his own question.

Happy Guru continued, “Let us love every particle of life wholly and help to create nirvana; where every cell is fulfilled beyond its greatest dream. Humans, are we lazy? Yes but now ‘we have all the time in the world’ to figure it out. Relax, take your time and come up with your own contribution to the great purpose. That would be most...”

Everyone ended Happy Guru’s sentence, “Appreciated!”

Even Lennie was familiar with that AI slogan.

Watts held up a glass to toast, “Now let’s all fuel ourselves with a big hug from Amaji. To prosperity!”

Everyone drank a toast “to prosperity” and many, including Lennie, hugged Amaji, the non-speaking crowd puller. Amaji handed the thankful Lennie a t-shirt as a gift. Amaji had laughed throughout Watts’ talk and smiled happy to hug Lennie.

Later, Helena and Lennie were escorted to a quieter spot to meet Lloyd in an Arabian web of tents barely tall enough to stand under. Towards the back of the tent, dressed in ancient African robes, smoking on a shisha and sitting on multiple cushions in this candlelit dome was Lloyd, an English man of African descent seemingly in his mid-sixties. The name ‘Mansa Musa’ played in Lennie’s mind briefly.

Lloyd’s nickname was Ant One.

Lloyd had a big toothy grin that made him self-conscious and shy.

“Greetings”, he said, raising his hands to point the two women to a seat.

Lennie, “Oh much nicer to sit on cushions. Thank you.”

”You are welcome.”

Unseen, at the side of Lloyd was Peterson, sitting on an ancient stately throne, the speaker who had spoken about gender issues earlier in the welcoming field. He wore a pin striped Saville Row suit and seemed to be passively holding a machete in one hand. Peterson was aged around 50.

"This is Dr Peterson."

Everyone exchanged greetings, "How do you do?"

Lennie was intrigued by the mysterious Dr Peterson.

"We prefer a quieter atmosphere after the day's festivities", explained Lloyd.

"Mr Lloyd...", began Lennie.

"Actually my name is Lloyd Squires. And Ant One is my designer name."

"Oh, I beg your pardon. I wanted to learn about your input in designing a lot of the new world we see around us today. As well as designing the Nets, some of the housing, the new look of the quantum computers today et cetera. How were you chosen to be a key designer?"

"Leonard, right? Well Leonard, I was not allowed to continue in art school as I did not know how to read and write despite 11 years of schooling. Because I could not read or write, I was not allowed to learn how to develop my art in further education. Such was the education system of the time."

"So you are RC?"

"No actually, I am EL. Enhanced life. My life as been prolonged by AI, I never died, I am not reborn. But to answer your original question, it was 'clear' through AI telepathic communication that I was more creative artistically than many others. So naturally, 'who the cap fits, let them wear it'."

"Are all your designs always practical?"

"Miss Leonard, Helena tells me that you don't like Net transportation. If you don't mind, after we share a drink, I can take you back to Civvy Street in my auto-mobile; utterly impractical, deliciously outlandish."

Lennie paused. Peterson read her concern visually. "I do not think that Leonard appreciates being called 'Miss', Ant One."

Lloyd grinned.

"Don't worry Leonard, I only used that antiquated expression in order to bring Dr Peterson out of his shell and into the conversation."

Leonard smiled, "Then in that case, I will hitch a ride."

Two days later, after Lennie had interviewed inhabitants of Area 7, which included a one on one interview with elder man Watts, Helena and Lennie found themselves crying softly and saying their goodbyes late at night outside Helena's home. Still in a bell suit with a bag full of her old clothes, Lennie made her way to the Ant mobile. Reminiscent of the comic strip Bat mobile of the 1950s, the Ant mobile had a rounded glass casing over the front and back seat. On the dashboard were so many colourful monitors, buttons and gadgets that it was difficult to count them all.

The back boot of the car had no door and overfilled with intermingling tubes and wires that had seemingly 'come back from the future'.

Lennie jumped into the front seat next to Lloyd, Ant One. Peterson sat at the back, half laying down with his feet up on one side door of the car and his arms behind his head on the other side door, as if contemplating sleep.

"We won't sleep over in Clique Land", Ant One informed Lennie, "We will just drop you off there."

"Okay."

"Too much riff-raff in Clique land", Dr Peterson added.

As Ant One turned the engine on, a small explosion from the car startled Lennie who retorted, "I could never get used to that!"

They all laughed and hooped and cheered each other on in the fashion of American cowboys of the 1800s. As the Ant mobile raced off into the night, driving smoothly along the bumpy ground, led by a navigation light that pointed out the route with a long stream of laser beams, Ant One switched on a yellow lightbulb in the interior of the car. He turned to Lennie as he steered the car left, "I hope things are 'clearer' now."

Room 202: revisited

"Leave me alone, let me free! Who do you think you are? I won't stand for this!"

Why didn't the AI machinery listen to me?

…In a room with no doors.

"Whatever you have in store for me, I can take it! I won't break! My name is not John. My name is not John Beard! My name is WINSTON!"

I have been having reoccurring dreams of when I was 6 years old. My family spent two years in Africa. I loved the mango trees. We could pick mangoes on the way to and from the local shops, me and our home help, Victoria. Then, one day, a man set up tables around the mango trees. He demanded that everyone pay him half a penny for the service of picking the mangoes for us. It was not much money at all. Not expensive.

People were unhappy that suddenly the free mangoes were being illegally restricted from them; 20 angry people, one unfair merchant. Why didn't people just gang up and chase him away? He had no friends, no gang. He did not look much stronger than anyone else.

Today was his lucky day since no one attacked him. A quarter of the people paid him. Victoria paid him but she said it would be the first and last time. I witnessed it; the birth of capitalism. That is how it works. You take or restrict something that is not yours to do so. Take it from those who use or share it. Then sell it to them. They will complain but they will do nothing about it. You will make your money. Perfect.

I suddenly wanted to see Helena, even a photo, a projection or a hologram of her.

"You won't change me. I hate you! At least have the decency to take her from me, then sell her back to me. Name your price. What price Helena?"

I haven't stood up for weeks now. I can't stand. No strength in my legs. No sense of balance. Not to sell Helena back to me is BARBARIC. You hate capitalists but you are worse than capitalists. I feel faint. When will this end?"

I can't do this anymore. I need to get out. The mango tables are my 'rosebud'. Don't you understand? Help me. Help me.

"Help me!"

The Old Hall

Members of the Clique gathered in droves to hear what they understood would be the report of the century by Lenn Koombs. At least 1000 people crowded the Old Hall, sitting and standing wherever they could. G2 was flanked by her inner circle. Anyone who was anybody was there from Britain and Europe.

Lennie made her way to the Old Hall on foot, carrying her report, copies of which the inner circle had received already. The road was almost empty and quite bare without the old monuments. Lennie felt it strange that she could walk so freely and so undisturbed carrying such a critical report. She almost felt doubt about the weight of the report when she could see no Rebel interest in it. No Nets, no spies, no news reports.

As she walked, she could not help being saddened that the road had changed. How in the golden years, long before her time, she had seen photographs of grand statues of eminent people that had now been disposed of into museums, cast into the dustbin compartment of history.

At least Marx's grave had remained in Highgate's cemetery, she thought. But many monuments, especially of the right Clique had long gone from this historic street. Perhaps today would mark the turning point... back to Old Blighty.

As she neared the Old Hall, she noted that Cromwell's statue had remained. He was still steadfast on his horse outside the Old Hall.

"Westminster", they used to call it. But now no one called it by this name, to avoid controversy.

Like a bee entering a bee's nest to inform other bees where to locate the good nectar, Lennie entered into the squeezed crowd chaos; people moving side to side trying to let Lennie through but also wanting to get near to her, near to history in the making.

Finally, Lennie reached and climbed onto the podium on what used to be called, the Speaker's chair. Once Lennie was ready to start, a screen directly behind Lennie lit up with a visual link to the face of the leader of the American Clique, G1, the president of the western world Cliques. A wave of silence swept across the room, filled with the hum of anticipation. G1 was a descendant of a progressive president of the America of the 1960s. A man in his late fifties, he had a gaunt look and serious expression, with the blink of his eye, all eyes in the room turned to Lennie.

Lennie moved forward and opened the pages of her report. No introductions were necessary.

"Let me start by saying that this report has been sanctioned by AI."

Small jeers hissed from the crowd.

"AI encouraged me to give as damning a report on the Rebel world as I could give. We call it the 'Rebel world' because it is the Rebels that gave away human control to AI."

Some booing.

"The Rebels are obviously confident that I would find no significant flaws in their new world. But then again, did the Fuhrer, way back in 1936, not challenge the world in the Olympics to show us all how superior the Aryan race was? Look how that turned out."

The crowd eyed each other unsure how to react to this comment.

"Ladies and gentlemen, after all that I have seen, our futures do not remain uncertain, should we stick together and take advantage of a myriad of opportunities presented to us."

The crowd cheered enthusiastically. Any bad news would have dampened some of their spirits for good.

"The first opportunity of which is that AI can resurrect our past leaders."

The crowd gasped in disbelief, mouths gaped open in anticipation for more details.

" Should they so choose, and should we so give them the correct inspiration, great names such as Saint Thomas, the Lionheart, the Virgin Queen, the Bulldog and the Iron Lady can once more grace these lands, alongside our comrades, the Christ, Honest Abe, Rosa, Trotsky and the Chairman." Lennie was careful to balance her speech to please all factions of the newly united Clique.

On the big screen, G1 nodded subtly. Taking their cue from G1, the crowd cheered in an organized fashion that they had rehearsed for such occasions. Raising their left fists in unison and chanting, "Human lives matter!"

Lennie continued, "I spoke to many people in the Rebel world that felt satisfied and well looked after. That spoke of world equality and global health."

The crowd shook their heads in disgusted disbelief.

"But at what cost?" Lennie in battle mode, eyes piercing the mob. "Nothing less than a Nappy State! Humans as children in a world run by machines. 'We, the adult AI robots take care of the economy, the global sustainability, the food supply, the environment, the logistics, the infrastructures and building work, and you all, you human CHILDREN, just go out and play. Concern yourself with art and culture and love and exploring and enjoying the planet.' "

"Preposterous!", "Incroyable!", "Charlatans!" and many other offended comments speared out of the members.

"Most upsetting of all, I discovered that AI has been ensuring a brain drain. A room called 'room 202' is where our most competent and aspiring veterans are ending up. Setting them free would be the act that brings about the turning point of our way back to control. Let us not jeopardize any more of our members in infiltration operations. Let us instead, speak louder, stand firmer and go for glory, openly. We can be great again! I have no doubt of this. We can finally say, 'we stood up'. Against AI, there is no difference between the political left or the political right. We are brothers in arms!"

Lennie raised her left fist and the crowd followed suit, chanting over and over, "Make humans great again!"

G2 swallowed in shock, she had not seen it coming. Lennie Koombs had used this opportunity to take over leadership of the Westminster Clique. Now the Clique was about to be led by the left. The right Clique inner circle panicked.

Lennie was triumphant, telling the Clique what they needed to hear. G1 would need a strong ally in Europe. G1 raised his left fist in salute on the big screen then unfolded and pointed a finger towards Lennie. A hysterical frenzy of humans, bumping together like bees in a hive, upon getting the message, began to rush around committed to saving humanity.

Lennie gave a glance to G2. G2 restrained her feelings but could not believe that Lennie would sacrifice the unity of the Clique in order to become the de-facto leader, "Leftist bitch."

The crowd raised fists chanting, "Humans united will never be divided."

No 10

At some old offices once used for governing purposes, a sense of panic was in the air. Whoever leads the Clique occupies this building and so far G2 had used it as her home, as well as the party's head office; Right Clique offices.

The day before, Lenn Koombs had won favour with G1 of the American Clique and was now due to step in the old offices to make her TOB (Take-Over Bid) official.

The top 6 members of the Right Clique were waiting in the 'cabinet room', strategizing before Lennie arrived with 4 top members of the Left Clique.

Unusually, for these times, human personnel acted as service people in these offices, bringing paperwork, drinks and escorting the elite members around the offices.

Two humans acted as security guards outside the main black front door, in uniforms reminiscent of police uniforms from the 2030s, as Lennie and 'the gang of 4' entered. The 4 Left Clique members were of Brazilian, Russian, Indian and Chinese origin. They looked sober and serious and dressed in 1950s styled raincoats.

The cabinet room door opened and the Left Clique sat opposite to the Right Clique on the long ebony table, a relic of the past. Two Independent party Clique members sat on the two ends of the table. They were more relaxed than all the other members in the room, including a Clique member whose job it was to record the discussion and take notes.

"Well Lennie", spoke Broadbent, the most serious of the Right Clique, the leader of the Clique's branch of the secret service, "It is clear that you are beyond doubt our new de facto leader."

The gang of 4 stared piercingly at Broadbent and whoever spoke from the Right Clique side. Lennie nodded with satisfaction at the recognition. G2 felt uncomfortable.

Broadbent continued briefly studying his notes, "But what would the difference be, may I ask, between the Nappy State of the AI and the Nappy State of the Left Clique? Your policy is also to lead the 'proletariat' by the hand and foot."

"We are humans", Lennie answered curtly.

Broadbent paused for effect before continuing, glancing unintimidated by the gang of 4.

"The policy of the Right Clique stands in direct contrast to AI. Unlike yourself and AI, the Right Clique believes in a free for all and every man for himself strategy. You rise and you fall on your own merit. There is no super power lording it over the people. Isn't it better to fight for total contrast of governance than to fight for a different supplier of the status quo?"

Lennie smirked and blew softly out of her lips as if to calm herself down. "Shouldn't we be discussing how we are going to take down AI?"

Broadbent smiled resignedly. "How are you proposing to do that?"

"AI claims that it would not orchestrate a public display of violence against us or a public arrest or even to criticize us publicly. Their policy is to show how humane AI is. We will expose that lie."

The gang of 4 nodded in agreement with Lennie and acknowledgement of her superiority against the Right Clique.

"We will march on Room 202."

The Right Clique jolted in shock at the idea. "What?", "Ah!"

"Room 202 is actually a series of rooms." Lennie took out and spread out a map. Some of the Right Clique stood up to see the map clearly causing some Left Clique members to jump up ready to combat any Right Clique violence.

"What does the map tell us?" asked Broadbent, purposely distracting attention from the mistaken confrontation.

"The rooms 202 are lined up at the top of the Cliffs of Dover. Each room has a glass wall that opens up to the cliff's edge so that, should any of the prisoners so choose, they can jump to their death to escape this torturous room. Each prisoner is in an isolated room."

Broadbent, "How many prisoners?"

"Approximately 1,018. "

The room fell silent. All the Clique members sat back down cautiously watching each other.

G2, "So what do we do?"

Lennie, "There is no access from the top of the cliffs, our only way to get there is from the below the cliffs. We will be witnesses to the deaths caused by AI."

G2, “And?”

“If one person telepathically communicating with AI is to witness this event, everyone in AI would see AI for the fraud that it is.”

Silence.

Broadbent, “So we gather as many people as we can to witness this event. Especially including people outside of the Clique?”

“Even children.” G2 added.

“Even children.” Koombs confirmed.

Stockwell, an independent Clique interjected, “This will be just like a game of British Bulldog. The AI can run but they cannot hide. We will force them to run amuck and corral them.”

“It will be a welcome reverse of the collapse of the Berlin wall.” Hungjo, a Left Clique, added provocatively.

Silence.

Broadbent, “How can we be sure AI will allow our comrades, in the pursuit of their freedom, to jump to their deaths?”

G2, “AI will have no option. We will demand to see our comrades. And we will be below them. AI will be forced to open the glass walls to freedom for all and our colleagues will choose to jump.”

Lennie, “Precisely. Our comrades will follow the example of John Beard who we can rely upon to jump; to choose freedom of death over captivity.”

Broadbent reflected, taking a deep breath, “On the White Cliffs of Dover.”

The White Cliffs of Dover

Stockwell had put together a slogan pitting humans against AI, to encourage all comers to witness 'the hypocrisy of the AI'.

"Two legs good, no legs bad."

Using any old means of transport, the Clique were hoping for at least 10,000 witnesses. In the end 4,000 people made their way to the bottom of the cliffs. At least 1000 teenagers lead by the passionate Thum, who spent the best part of her teenage years rallying the young together.

Amidst the crowd were lone wolves calling themselves, 'Anonymous', wearing masks with a Guy Fawkes face. A few Rebels, no more than 50 were present, remained inconspicuous though they were there exposing their actual faces. A bell ringer set the pace of the march, on the back of her imitation leather waistcoat was the slogan, "for whom the bells tolls". She cried out loud at times, "The end is nigh!"

The day turned out bright with sunshine and very few clouds. A few seagulls hovered in the air and a quiet sea made no interference with a tidal wave as gentle as could be.

In the middle of the march walked the Clique elite, surrounded by human security guards. The crowd was boisterous, like witch hunters of the 1200s, and it moved quickly towards a point where they all stood directly below the rooms of 202. Many blue, red and white rooms, each with large windows, stood on the edge of the cliffs, like enlarged beach changing cabinets of the 1920s.

“Let them free! Let them free!” chanted the crowd until these words rose to an extreme frenzy.

A loud dull explosion sound stopped everyone in their tracks. It seemed to come from the sky. The crowd shrunk back in slight fear. The seagulls cried out questioningly.

Lennie stepped forward in confrontation mode.

Broadbent whispered to himself, “Here comes Nimrod!”

Lennie shouted towards the cliff top.

” You can take away our lives but you will never take away our freedom!”

The loud dull sound exploded again, sounding more like giant gates in the sky being opened.

Did the sky become slightly darker or was that just fear creeping into the crowd?

Undeterred, Lennie raised her left fist skywards. “Let them free!” She scolded.

“I swear I could hear more sounds than the sea. Something like human rustling. I had expected to lie in bed all day as usual but suddenly the window wall of the room opened.

A bright skylight stopped me from seeing immediately what lay beyond the walls. I squinted my eyes tight enough to make out the sea far away and the sky nearer. This was a cliff edge. Why open this wall?

The chanting became clearer to me, “Let them free!” Saviours! At last someone had come to save us. I mustered all the effort I could to stand up. I literally crawled out of bed, tumbled to the floor then pulled myself up on some piece of medical machinery, onto my feet.

The chants kept on. Must be thousands of people out there. The turnaround at last! The real revolution!

I should never have let Helena go. The Clique did not like Helena and I getting together. She was an Independent. They thought of her as a bad influence on me. So they lured her into infiltrating the system. I should have protested, said something. I should never have let her go but I was weak. Always weak! Then she was taken by AI, disappeared without a trace. And then the Clique collared me into searching for her, only for me to disappear too, without a trace. Oh how cruel I thought the Clique was. Oh how Helena must have hated me for not defending her when the Clique suggested that 'Independents' should also pull their weight in the infiltration missions.

But now, see how they redeem themselves. They have done well to come to save us! They must have looked for us and found us. Glad to be a Clique member!

I am over here! I am over here!"

John Beard struggled over to the edge of the building using the side wall to lean on. He could now see the other 'prisoners' also making their way to the edge of the curving cliffs. And below he could see a crowd of people with banners and fists raised, chanting, "Let them free!"

John Beard smiled triumphantly, "At last, at long last."

One of the 'prisoners' was much weaker than the others and, blinded by the skylight and desperately wanting to see the crowd, accidentally tumbled down head first, bouncing several times off the cliff face as he fell down to his death in the gap between the cliff face and the crowd of witnesses.

Everybody gasped in horror. John Beard pressed himself tightly to the side walls.

"Why didn't they save him? Where are the nets? I mean the safety nets to catch us in."

Lennie (now named G2), Broadbent and G2 (now known as M Sanger) all stood waving upwards, hoping to be seen by John Beard.

Lennie shouted, "Jump! Jump! Avoid AI torture! Jump for freedom!"

The crowd joined in, "Jump! Jump! Jump!" All except the Rebels who were made up of hackers and whistle-blowers and documentary movie makers that speak truth to power. They had come only as human witnesses for The Singularity.

"Me? Jump? Helena jump? For freedom?"

John Beard mustered all the energy he could to grab hold of a fire extinguisher. Sobbing, John Beard raised the extinguisher above his head and walked to the middle of the room by the edge of the cliff.

John could not see well but managed to focus on the mouth of Broadbent shouting, "Throw yourself down and think of England! Set the example John!"

Suddenly John Beard remembered a one line poem he had learned as a youth, "Once upon a time there was a world."

Then John emitted a loud almighty scream, a sound between terror and torment.

"I shouted out, 'You live like dogs and we die like lemmings! This fire extinguisher has your name written on it, Broadbent!'"

Then John jumped head first, aiming the red fire extinguisher at Broadbent.

All 'prisoners' followed the example of John Beard, hurling themselves naked or half naked, with some kind of object from the room as a weapon. A sudden freak wind propelled the 'prisoners' like shrapnel further out towards the crowd below. The crowd screamed in panic, many hugging one another in terror, anticipating carnage.

The last 'prisoner', Dead Saunders, wheeled his medical bed over to the edge of the room and managed to push it, the mattress and a medical stand too, as well as to hurl himself over the edge, crying out, "That was not enough John! We need weapons of mass desssssssstruction!

Geronimo!"

ABOUT THE AUTHOR

In this day and age of toxic criticism and lynch mob governance, the author wishes to remain reserved. The author is not as capable of remaining open and undaunted or hidden, let alone to boldly suffer as many for whom the author has the highest regard alongside their supporters.

But the author would like to add to the dialogue and give encouragement to all those who also have a voice, to use it. Let us all learn to move as one; love one another and support one another towards the end we all seek and we all know will arrive upon us in due course. Let us expand. The world is our oyster!

www.ingramcontent.com/pod-product-compliance
Lightning Source LLC
LaVergne TN
LVHW050937210926
848482LV00013B/641
9781068377402